15 Businesses You Can Start with Little or No Cash

Danny Tucker

Contents

Contents 1

A Message from the Author 2

Introduction 3

Why Start Your Own Business? 4

15 Businesses You Can Start with Little or No Cash 5

Janitorial Service 6

Window Washing 8

Lawn Care 10

Sidewalk Washing 12

Cleaning and Hauling 14

Auto Detailing 15

Window Tinting 17

Construction Site Cleanup 18

Buying and Selling 19

Advertising Specialties 21

Parking Lot Painting 22

Home Insulating 24

Painting 26

Chimney Sweeping 29

Turnkey Rental Unit Spruceup 31

Building Your Business 33

Three years ago, when my wife and I left Arkansas, we had $250 in our pockets and every material possession we owned in a small U-Haul trailer hitched to our vehicle.

Today, we enjoy a healthy income working about six hours a day (sometimes less). How did we get from there to where we are today? By starting our own business.

You'll find out more about that business in Chapter 15 of this book. You'll also read about 14 other businesses that are equally easy to start and can be equally profitable.

The business we started was a turnkey rental unit spruce-up business. Our only investment was $50 in business cards and the time we spent knocking on doors to spread word of our service.

At first, all we got were the "crumbs," the business that similar services didn't want. But within weeks of starting our business, we got our first break: The manager of an apartment unit in our town was dissatisfied with the outfit currently cleaning her units, so she agreed to give us a try.

I'll never forget that apartment. It took my wife and I 19 hours to paint the walls, shampoo the carpet, and give the place a thorough cleaning. (Today, we can perform the same work in three hours.) We were so excited when we got our first check!

The apartment manager was pleased with our work, so she started calling us when other apartments were vacated. We proved that we were responsive, reliable, and thorough.

As a result, we were given a contract on two additional complexes. We were in business! We're living proof that it's possible to earn a decent living without attending college, without slaving 10 hours a day for someone else, and without incurring great financial risk.

All it takes is the desire, the willingness to work hard (at least in the beginning), and the persistence to stick with it until you've established yourself. Oh, it takes one more thing: You must always, always do quality work.

All the desire and persistence in the world won't help you if your work is shoddy or haphazard. Do the job—every job—right.

So...if my story has inspired you, and you think you have what it takes, read on. Your new life is about to begin!

Congratulations! By purchasing this book, you've taken the first step on the exciting and challenging road to owning your own business. You're about to discover more than a dozen businesses you can start—simply and inexpensively—without a college degree, without years of experience, and without draining your savings or mortgaging your house.

The businesses described in this book were chosen from hundreds of business opportunities because they have the following characteristics:

- Strong earning potential
- Easy entry
- Simple operation
- Little or no startup costs

These businesses were also chosen because they require no special skills, education, or experience. But that doesn't mean you should plunge in blindly. Remember, this book is designed to give you ideas and genera] information only. Before you launch a business of your own, do your homework. Make phone calls. Talk to people in similar or related fields in your own or nearby towns. Ask questions. Get answers.

Done correctly, these businesses can put a substantial amount of money in your pocket--in most cases, far more money than you can earn working for someone else. More importantly, they can get you out of the nine-to-five rut—or the unemployment line--and put you in control of your life and future.

The reasons people start their own businesses are as varied as people themselves. Here are a few of the most common:

> ➢ To escape a frustrating job. Many people start their own business because they're unhappy in their current job. You may want to escape a pain-in-the-neck boss, or irritating co-workers. Maybe your job keeps you in a state of constant stress. Or maybe it isn't challenging enough. By starting your own business, you can become your own boss. You choose the people you work with. Because you're in control, you'll experience far less stress. And because you determine the business you'll be in, you can choose one that excites and challenges you.

> ➢ To supplement your income from your present job. You may like your current job but want or need additional income--for your kid's education, for retirement, or for those little extras in life. Many of the businesses described in this book can be started part time—mornings, evenings, or on weekends. So you can continue your present job but boost your earnings.

> ➢ To-escape unemployment. Few things are more terrifying or demoralizing than pounding the pavement in search of a job. Starting your own business puts an end to that. No more cover letters. No more applications. No more interviews. You can start working—and earning a paycheck—now.

> ➢ To launch a post-retirement career. Perhaps you've recently retired and discovered that a life of leisure isn't as wonderful as you thought it would be. Starting your own business can give you an outlet for your experience and maturity, while adding a lot more "gold" to your golden years.

> ➢ To gain more control over your life and time. As a business owner, you set your own hours. You don't have to ask someone's permission to take a day off. You don't have to phone in to an unsympathetic boss when you're sick. You determine when and how much you'll work.

Despite the many benefits of owning your own business, you should not walk up to your boss tomorrow and quit your job. Instead, start slowly. All the business opportunities in this manual can be done on a part-time basis.

If, on the other hand, you're unemployed, as so many people are these days, you have nothing to lose. Pick a business and get going! It may well be the smartest move you've ever made.

But don't procrastinate. Please, don't order this manual and then let it lie around and collect dust. Pick a business and then get out there and do it! You'll see a big improvement in your life, in your confidence level—and in your bank balance!

15 Businesses You Can Start with Little or No Cash

Tools and Equipment Needed:

- o Cell phone with voicemail service turned on
- o Cleaning supplies (window, bath, and wood cleaners)
- o Brooms (push and regular)
- o Dust mop
- o Wet mop and bucket
- o Buffer
- o Carpet cleaner
- o Bid forms
- o Receipt book

There is big money to be made in the janitorial business, and it doesn't cost a lot to get started. Many places that use this type of service already have the necessary equipment. If they don't, you can always rent until you can afford to buy.

The one drawback to this business (to some) is that it requires working evening hours or some weekends. On the other hand, if you're looking to supplement your current income from your day job or to start your own business part-time, this type of schedule can be ideal.

Before you set out to get that first job, you'll need information. One of the best ways to get it is to actually go to work for a janitorial service in your area.
Then observe:
What kind of equipment is available and how do you use it'? (Vacuum cleaners are easy but do you know how to use a floor polishing machine? A carpet cleaner?) What cleaning solutions are used for what? What's usually expected from janitorial services'? How does the company price its services?

After just a month or two of this type of work, you should have answers to all your questions. And you'll feel much more confident about jumping out on your own.

Cleaning experts behind the desk of janitorial supply companies are another great source of information. You can find these companies in online or in the Yellow Pages. Tell the pros there that you're starting a janitorial business and could use a little advice. They should be more than happy to help you. After all, you are a future customer!

Now, where do you find this type of work? Simply look around you. Every professional building you see has to be cleaned. Office buildings and medical facilities must be cleaned daily. Factories often use a janitorial service to keep their offices, restrooms, and breakrooms clean. Many large department stores and grocery stores use janitorial services. And malls are major consumers of janitorial services. (But wait until you're a seasoned pro to take on jobs this size.)

Once you've made a list of places you feel you may be interested in your service, go see the office or building managers. Tell them you're launching a janitorial service in the area and would like to give them a bid. If they accept your invitation, prepare your bid carefully.

Tour the facility and note what would be involved in keeping it clean. Ask questions. What surfaces have to be cleaned? How many trash cans must be emptied? Does the waste need special handling and disposal? (Medical waste often does.) How many bathrooms are there and how big are they? What about cooking and eating areas? How often must windows and doors be cleaned? Write down the answers to these questions and refer to the information when you're preparing your bid.

If the building manager says he already has a contract with another service, ask when that contract expires. Note that date of your calendar and make it a point to call back a few weeks before that date to offer a bid. If he's not completely satisfied, he may be ready to change services.

All your bids should be submitted on a professional bid form. You can find these at your local office supply store, or they can be printed inexpensively by your local printer. Don't be disappointed when you don't get every job. You won't. Just keep prospecting and bidding.

Once you've gotten those first jobs, you'll want to develop a system that gets you in and out of the building as quickly as possible yet gets the job done. So take some time to plan your approach. For example, how will you carry your cleaning supplies? Some people purchase an apron with pockets or loops that hold cleaning supplies in ready reach. Others prefer plastic carriers to tote cleaning solutions and rags from room to room. You'll also need to decide how you'll "work the room." In general, you'll want to clean from the top down, and from the side of the room opposite the door forward, so you don't walk on the area you've just cleaned. Your nearby library or multiple online sites probably have a number of books/information on cleaning. Check them out.

By the way, this is a great business for a husband and wife team. Having two people on the job cuts your time on the site in half. And wives are always thrilled to see their husband wielding a mop for a change!

Tools and Equipment Needed:

- o Cell phone with voicemail service turned on
- o Bucket
- o Cleaning solution
- o Long-handled pole
- o Scrub brush attachment
- o Squeegee attachment
- o Razor scraper
- o Ladder
- o Rags or paper towels
- o Receipt book

This business is inexpensive to launch and can be quite profitable. You can easily earn $20 an hour or more.

To start, you should become a first-rate window washer. Practice on your own windows and those of your friends. Offer a one-time-only free window cleaning to businesses in your area. (They may become your first customers!) Practice with your squeegee until you can handle it like a pro.

However, you learn your trade, learn to do it fast and well. Professional window washers are good, and if you're going to succeed you'll need to match their skills and speed as closely as possible.

Once you've mastered your craft, determine your rates. Pricing may vary from city to city, so you'll need to check around. Try calling a few window washers in your area. Pretend you're a store owner and ask what they would charge to clean a six-by-four window. Use their quote as a guide for pricing your own services.

If you're unable to discover the going rate by talking to people already in the business, try basing your charges on how long a job takes. Once you've gotten past the learning curve, time how long it takes you to clean windows of various sizes. Multiply that by your hourly rate and you've got your price.

Once you've gotten the skills and you know how much to charge for your service, your next step is finding customers. Placing newspaper ads, attaching magnetic signs on your vehicle, distributing flyers, and posting notices on bulletin boards are tried-and-true methods of announcing your availability. But the most effective way to market this business is to simply go door-to-door in the business section of your town and talk to store and

office managers and owners. (Strip malls, with their multitude of store fronts, can be a real gold mine!) Tell the managers and owners that you "do windows." If necessary, remind them that dirty windows obscure merchandise displays and make their business look unprofessional.

Explain that you offer quality work that's guaranteed and that you're dependable. You might offer a free window cleaning for first-time customers to demonstrate the quality of your work.

Don't be discouraged if you don't find work your first day out. Keep trying. The more people you talk to, the better your odds of finding customers.

Remember that repeat business IS just as important as new business. Try to set your customers up on a weekly, biweekly, or monthly schedule. This ensures them of clean windows, and it ensures you of steady work.

If you're uncomfortable with the selling aspect of this business, you might let someone else call on prospective customers and pay them on a commission basis for the businesses they sign up. But keep in mind that this can cut into your earnings.

Want to expand your profits even more? Offer window washing for homes as well as businesses. This can be particularly profitable in early spring, when after a dreary winter homeowners are eager to let the sun shine in!

Tools and Equipment Needed:

- o Cell phone with voicemail service turned on
- o Lawn Mower
- o String trimmer
- o Leaf rake
- o Push broom or blower
- o Safety goggles
- o Lawn and leaf bags
- o Truck or trailer
- o Receipt book

If you're a home owner, you probably have plenty of experience in this line of work! The most time-consuming aspect of lawn care—and the backbone of most lawn care businesses--is mowing. How do you find out the going rate for lawn mowing in your area?

Try calling other mowing services and ask for an estimate on the cost of mowing your own lawn. Another way to determine your rate is to calculate how long a job is likely to take and base your price on that. You might under- or overbid at first, but eventually you'll get good at estimating.

Once you have some idea of what to charge, you're ready for your first customers. How do you get them? Classified ads, magnetic signs on your vehicle, and notices on bulletin boards usually work. You can also attach flyers with information about your service on mailboxes or doorknobs in your community. (Don't put the flyers inside the mailboxes. U.S. Postal Service regulations prohibit the insertion of anything but official mail. Otherwise boxes might get too full to hold the mail!)

Once your business is up and rolling, word of mouth will carry news of your work-- good or bad. So when you get those first customers, be sure they're satisfied. Don't hesitate to ask happy customers if they know of other homeowners who need expert lawn care. If you've done your job well, they won't mind giving you a list of friends and relatives or telling their neighbors about you. They might even give you a letter of reference, which you can then post online or copy and distribute in the neighborhood.

One of the best places to find commercial lawn care work is through real estate companies. Realtors, who are often property managers as well, frequently require this type of service to maintain their properties. Apartment complexes and condos also need lawn care, as do many office and medical complexes. Any business with grass is a potential customer.

Now, about equipment: If you're serious about lawn care, you'll eventually want to purchase professional mowing equipment. But that usually isn't necessary in the beginning.

Start with what you have, and work your way up as your profits allow. That goes for blowers too. Start with a broom if you have to and purchase a blower as soon as you can afford it.

Remember, lawn care equipment can be destructive as well as beneficial to lawns and plants. Be extremely careful when mowing and trimming around trees, shrubs, and flowers. Mowers can make mincemeat of flower beds in seconds, and string trimmers can be lethal to trees if you allow the string to cut into the bark. So be careful. Replacing mature landscaping plants you've damaged can quickly wipe out your profits!

Remember too that lawn care equipment can be hazardous to humans as well as plants. Protect yourself from flying debris by wearing protective eye wear and long pants on the job. And make sure homeowners, kids, and pets are clear of your work area. You don't want them to be struck by debris either.

One of the biggest drawbacks to running a lawn care business is that you sometimes have to work in searing heat. You could schedule your jobs in the morning or late afternoon. But what if you want to work the entire day? You can. Thanks to modern ingenuity, you can now buy special vests that can be filled with ice and buckled on like a life jacket to keep you cool even on the hottest days. Check with army surplus and camping supply stores in your area.

Want to expand your lawn care service into Fall? Then take note that in autumn lawn care turns to leaf removal. Grab your rake and blower, strap a grass catcher onto your mower, and you're ready to cash in on lawn care right into November.

Then, of course, comes winter snow (and snow shoveling), followed by spring planting (which requires digging and mulching). Add it all up and you've got a year-round business. *Ain't Mother Nature wonderful!*

Tools and Equipment Needed:

- Cell phone with voicemail service turned on
- Cleaning solutions
- Brushes
- Scrapers
- Broom
- Receipt book

If you've looked at the sidewalks around you lately you'll know: This is a sorely neglected part of building maintenance. In front of department stores, grocery stores, malls, schools, and office complexes—dirty, greasy, gummy sidewalks abound. Apartment breezeways could use a little attention too. That makes sidewalk washing a prime money-making opportunity! And it takes very little capital to get started.

First, you'll need cleaning equipment. The spray from an ordinary water hose will remove some of the grime. But to really power out ground-in dirt, you should consider purchasing a pressure washer. With an average 300 pounds of pressure per square inch, these machines can force out even the stubbornest gunk and restore blackened sidewalks to a just-poured brightness.

To minimize startup cost, you might want to consider renting a pressure washer instead of buying one. But whether you rent or buy, use caution. Make sure you adhere to all safety precautions and that you follow the manufacturer's directions to the letter.

You can boost the effect of a hose or pressure washer with the right cleaning solutions. Talk to the experts at janitorial supply companies in your town. They'll be happy to discuss the most appropriate products.

As with all businesses, it's important to look like a pro. Before you take that first job, purchase some supplies, get your hands on some equipment, and practice on the sidewalks in front of your house. If there aren't any, go to your kid's school and offer to clean the sidewalks for free. The school administration will be thrilled! And you'll get lots of experience in removing gum from concrete. Something you need to know how to do in this line of work!

Now, let's talk about pricing. Here's where those practice sessions come in handy again. As you're cleaning, mark off a carefully measured section, clean it, and note how long it took. Determine what your hourly rate will be, and you've got your price.

About marketing: Because this is an unusual service, it's important to let business owners know it's available. They're not likely to think of it on their own. Try placing ads on social media sites, or free online forums (a display ad would be great) and distributing flyers at businesses in your area. Or just talk to people who might be your customers. If possible, show them a few before and after pictures of sidewalks you've cleaned. They'll see the difference. You might also check with the appropriate government offices in your town or city. Officials just might be interested in contracting for your services for the entire downtown area!

With every customer you get, try to schedule routine cleanings, perhaps every three to six months, or at least once a year. Regular customers reduce the need for continual marketing to new prospects.

With a little initiative, you should soon have enough work to keep busy. Who could have known? A profitable business was right under your nose--or rather, your toes!

Tools and Equipment Needed:

- o Cell phone with voicemail service turned on
- o Shovel
- o Rake (iron)
- o Work gloves
- o Garbage bags
- o Truck or trailer

This can be a surprisingly profitable business. Yet it requires very little to get started and can make you money in more ways than one.

Many American home owners have garages, basements, attics, barns, and storage buildings that are stacked floor to ceiling with bicycles, old lamps, toys, furniture, tools, sports and exercise equipment, and other souvenirs of past lives and forgotten interests.

Those same home owners would probably love to have those spaces emptied and cleaned. That's where you come in. By taking care of this odious task, you not only earn money for the cleanup, you can often sell the stuff you haul off. It's like getting paid twice.

How much should you charge for this type of service? Generally, you should be able to get about $50 to $80 a load, depending on the size of your truck and how difficult the items are to load and haul. Also, disposal of some items—batteries and used oil, for example-requires that you pay a disposal fee. Check with personnel at dump sites about disposal fees before you give customers a quote.

Keep in mind too that many items you're asked to dispose of (paper, vehicle batteries, and items made of aluminum and some other metals) have recycle value and can boost your earnings. Check online or in the Yellow Pages under "Recycling Centers."

To get started in the cleaning and hauling business, place ads online in the classified section of your local newspaper under "Services Offered" or a similar heading or go to multiple marketplace sites. Create some flyers and post them on bulletin boards. Have a magnetic sign made for the side of your vehicle. Or simply go door-to-door in various communities, distributing flyers or business cards and talking to home owners.

Elderly people are particularly hospitable to this type of service. Because many of them have arthritis or other debilitating conditions, they may not be able to do the bending and lifting required and would be glad to have someone do it for them.

Work hard at this business and you'll see that truth of the old saying: One man's trash truly is another man's treasure!

Tools and Equipment Needed:

- o Cell phone with voicemail service turned on
- o Vacuum cleaner with attachments
- o Window cleaner
- o Vinyl cleaner
- o Car-washing liquid
- o Carpet and upholstery cleaner
- o Wax
- o Brushes (small and large)
- o Armor All (or other protectant-type product)
- o Towels
- o Receipt book

Auto detailing can make you a lot of money—and it doesn't require a big cash outlay. In fact, you probably already have almost everything you need to get started. Yet you can easily earn $100 to $200 per vehicle with an investment of only three to four hours.

As with other businesses, practice before you begin. Detail your own set of wheels—as well as those of your friends. What you're after is a spotless vehicle—inside and out. That means every surface has to be cleaned—dash, upholstery, windows, carpeting, even the trunk.

Note of caution: The ceiling inside vehicles—called the headliner—is usually nothing more than thin fabric glued to cardboard and is very fragile. Limit your cleaning efforts to a light sweep with a soft brush or a gentle vacuuming with an upholstery tool. Never put water on a headliner. The results can be disastrous!

The outside as well as the inside of the vehicle should be spotless, right down to the tires. You can purchase special tire cleaners (as well as cleaning solutions for other surfaces) at your local auto parts store. Tell the manager that you're starting a detailing business and will be purchasing products often and he may give you a discount.

A second note of caution: Be sure that you read the labels on the products you use carefully. The last thing you need is to the expense of repairing damage to a customer's vehicle.

This profession isn't called "detailing" for nothing. It requires just that: attention to detail. Make sure you clean every nook and cranny, even those little grooves alongside the gear shift and the hollows in the arm rests. Overlook nothing.

Although detailing requires little in the way of equipment, it does require a temperature- controlled space if it's to be year-round work. If you have an enclosed garage, you're in business. If not, see if you can negotiate a deal with the owner of a related business—a window tint shop, an oil and lube business, or a body shop, for example. This can be a 1 mutually beneficial arrangement.

(Hint: Auto detailing goes hand-in-hand with window tinting. If you have a reliable friend who's looking to start a window-tinting business, you might consider pooling your resources and leasing a space for both businesses.)

Once you've lined up your space, determine your rates. You can do this by making a few phone calls to learn the going rate in your area. Then set your price accordingly. Once you've gotten your location and determined your rates, you're ready to market your business. Visit the primary users of this service--car dealerships (new and used). Body shops are a good bet too. And don't forget individuals. People spend a lot of time in their vehicles nowadays. So they're willing to spend a few bucks to keep them in showroom condition.

Try to make every first-time customer a regular customer. Offer a discount to those individuals who bring their car in for detailing on a regular basis. You might consider coming up with a card that's punched or stamped every time the customer comes in. After a certain number of visits, the next detailing job could be free. Be creative and think of other ways to generate repeat business and your need to market yourself is minimized.

So, want to earn a good living? It's all in the "details"!

Tools and equipment needed:

- o Cell phone with voicemail service turned on
- o Tinting material
- o Tinting brush
- o Scrapers
- o Window cleaner

Have you ever had the windows of your vehicle tinted'? If so, you 're well aware of the money the pros make in an hour or two. I recently had four windows tinted on my car. The cost was more than $97.

But this service is growing in popularity, for several reasons. First, it eliminates the blinding glare that plagues drivers when they're facing direct sunlight. Second, it protects vehicle interiors from the fading and decomposition caused by bright sunlight. And third, it grants drivers and their passengers a measure of privacy from the prying eyes of others.

If you've never tinted windows before, you'll need some experience before you take on your first paying customer. Go to a nearby auto parts store and buy yourself some professional-grade tinting material. Practice on your own vehicle until you get the hang of it. For additional practice, see if friends or family members will allow you to tint their windows. They will probably gladly pay for the materials in exchange for having their windows tinted.

Charges for window tinting vary, and to determine what you should charge, make a few calls to existing window-tinting businesses in your area.

You're going to need a place to work. Your own garage or basement is a fine place to start. If it can be heated and cooled, you can do your work comfortably year-round. Eventually, you may want to lease a space for your tinting business. If so, be sure that you have a professionally designed sign outside your business. On a busy street, this may be all the advertisement you need. You might also want to consider contacting owners of related businesses (body shops, repair shops, detailers) and leasing a small area in which to work.

Now that you've settled on a space, you're ready to market yourself. In addition to going after the tinting business of individuals, you'll want to contact new and used car dealerships in your area. To entice them to give you a try, you might want to offer a discount on the first few vehicles.

You should also try placing classified ads in the newspaper, posting notices on bulletin boards, and distributing flyers.

By the way, the latest and most innovative approach to this service is to go mobile. All you need is a van with the name and nature of your business painted on the side (by a pro, please!). Stash your materials in back and you're ready to roll. And roll in the bucks!

Tools and Equipment Needed:

- o Cell phone with voicemail service turned on
- o Shovel
- o Rake
- o Broom
- o Cleaning solutions
- o Truck or trailer

Construction is messy work, and anytime a job is completed, there is inevitably cleanup work to be done. That means this is a prime money-making opportunity, particularly if you live in or near a fast-growing area.

What's involved in construction site cleanup? Essentially two steps. One, removing all leftover building materials and debris from the sight. And two, getting the building in ready-to-occupy order: cleaning cabinets and fixtures, dusting window ledges, removing decals from appliances and windows, vacuuming carpets, sweeping and mopping vinyl flooring, and so on.

One of the best ways to find this type of work is to go directly to the construction sites in your area and ask to speak to the contractor in charge. Introduce yourself and your service. Offer to give him a bid on the job.

If you're unable to catch the contractor on site, try to reach him by phone. You may be able to get a mobile phone number or beeper number from workers on the site. If not, try to call him at home in the evening or early morning. Once you've gotten him on the phone, don't waste time. Be polite, but to the point. If he's resistant to hearing your sales spiel, tell him you understand his reservations and ask if you could at least give him a bid. Then submit your bid on a professionally designed form. (Check your local office supply store for ready-made forms. If they don't have any, check online.)

Another way to get this type of work is to place a classified ad in the "Services Offered" section of newspapers. Be sure that you have a cell phone with voicemail service turned on to catch calls when you're not home.

What should you charge for this type of service? One to two hundred per house is typical. You should charge more for large or unusually dirty sites. Your rate should be based on how long you expect it to take to do the work.

Set aside at least a few days a month to contact contractors on a continual basis. Keep your name in the front of their minds, and when there's cleanup to be done, they'll think of you.

Tools and Equipment Needed:

- o   Cell phone with voicemail service turned on
- o   Truck or trailer
- o   Receipt book
- o   Storage space

This is an exciting way to earn a lot of money, and you can get started with as little as $20 to $30.

But first, a cautionary note: The secret of running a profitable buying and selling business is to buy merchandise inexpensively and resell it at a higher price. It's crucial that you know the current value of the items you choose to buy and sell. That's why many people decide to specialize in a particular type of item: toys, baby items, furniture, and so on. It's better to become knowledgeable about one type of merchandise and buy and sell it profitably than to know a little about many items and risk losing money.

Second, unless you're a Mr. (or Mrs.) Fix-it, be careful about buying non-working or "breakable" items such as appliances and lawn mowers. Stick with things that aren't mechanical.

Third, when deciding what you'll buy and sell, remember: you'll have a larger market if you buy and sell only those items that are needed by everyone—furniture, for example.

Finally, go slowly at first. Don't rush out and buy a big bunch of stuff. Two or three items are enough to get you started. And make sure the items are true bargains. You should double your money when you resell the items you buy.

Now, how do you find these bargains'? Yard sales are great sources. But be sure to look items over thoroughly and make sure they're in good condition before buying them.

Another pointer: Get there early, at least 30 minutes before the sale is scheduled to begin. The best buys disappear fast. Finally, offer the seller less than the asking price. He'll probably take it. Auctions are a great place to look for bargains too, and you'll find an auction somewhere just about every weekend. Check the "Auction" section of the classifieds online or in your local paper. Or call the folks listed in the Yellow Pages under "Auctioneers" or "Liquidators" and ask to be put on their mailing list.

Always get to an auction early. That way, you'll have time to examine the items for sale closely and decide how much you're willing to pay. Most auctioneers have a "preview" time or day in which you can look the merchandise over at a leisurely pace. If you're not familiar with how auctions work, go to a few and watch what's going on before you participate.

Where do you sell your bargains? Try placing on social mediaMany newspapers offer "freebie" ads for items below a certain price, say, $150. This allows you to put your item on the market with no cost, so if your newspaper offers this service, by all means take advantage of it.

Some radio stations have "swap and shop" shows that allow you to phone in a verbal ad for items you're offering for sale. These are also usually free.

You can also try using posting notices on bulletin boards at laundry mats, grocery stores, and apartment complexes. Describe your item completely (size, color, condition, etc.) and make sure your notice can be seen from a good distance away. Also, make it easy for prospects to get hold of you. Here's an idea. When you're creating your flyer, draw some vertical lines from the bottom of the page to a point about three inches up. Write your phone number between each of the lines and cut the lines with scissors. Prospective customers can easily tear off one of the little pieces of paper with your number and take it with them if they're interested in the item.

A third option is to use a consignment service. You leave your merchandise with a particular shop, they display the item or items for you and, with a little luck, sell it. In exchange for displaying the item, they take a portion of the selling price, usually somewhere between 30 and 60 percent. The disadvantage is, obviously, a cut into your profits. The advantage is that your merchandise is seen by more people than would ordinarily get to see it. And you don't have to bother with placing ads. Check your local Yellow Pages under the heading "Consignment Shops" to find stores that accept consigned merchandise.

Another place where you might resell your items is at a flea market. Flea market owners usually charge a daily, weekly, or monthly rate in exchange for which they'll allow you to display your merchandise. As with consignment shops, the advantage is that more people see your merchandise; the disadvantage is that your profits are pruned.

Buying and selling is not only a money-making business, it can be a heck of a lot of fun. There's nothing quite like the thrill of the hunt, of finding that great item for a ridiculously low price that you know you can double. You just have to find those bargains. So, get out there and find them! Happy hunting!

Tools and Equipment Needed:

- o   Cell phone with voicemail service turned on

Advertising specialties is a multifaceted business with lots of opportunities. Here's just one of the easy and fun ways you can get started in the advertising specialties business. Have you ever eaten in a restaurant that had paper place mats'? Did you notice that those place mats are usually covered with ads from local places or business'? I bet you're getting the picture already!

Visit the owners and managers of local restaurants in your area and let them know that you'll provide them with place mats free of charge. Once they've accepted your offer, go to businesses in your area and sell them a spot on your place mat. (Figure out ahead of time how many ads you'd like to put on the place mat and what size each ad will be. Don't crowd in too many ads or they'll lose their effectiveness.) Let them know that dozens of people—maybe hundreds, depending on the size of the restaurant—will see their ads every day and that this is an economical way to get their name in front of the public. Invite them to include a discount offer (of say, 10 to 20 percent off any purchase) that will encourage restaurant patrons to cut out the coupon and visit the business. Tell them this will give them a clear demonstration of how effective the ad can be, as they'll have the cut-out coupon as proof.

You should be able to sell ads on your place mats for between $25 to $200, depending on the market in your area.

Be creative in putting together your place mat layout. If possible, include a puzzle, quiz, or some type of game in one or both of the lower corners. (Save the top section for ads.)

Also, try to make your mat as attractive as possible. If you're not into desktop publishing, call the graphic design department of a nearby college and ask if they have a talented student who would do the work inexpensively. Or ask about design services at printing firms in your town. But do make sure your place mats have a professional look to them. This will make it easier for you to sell ad space.

Before you have your place mats printed, be sure that you get at least three bids from printers in your area. Prices can vary widely from one to another. Also, be sure to get the bid in writing. You don't want any surprises when it comes time to pay the bill.

If you're uncomfortable with the selling aspect of this business, you could pay someone a commission to call on your prospects. But remember, this can make inroads on your profits. Your best bet is to take a deep breath and make those sales calls yourself. It usually isn't a difficult sale, and once you've experienced a few successes--and a few good-size paychecks—your resistance to selling will probably disappear!

Tools and Equipment Needed:

- o Cell phone with voicemail service turned on
- o Push broom
- o Spray machine
- o Receipt book

Think about this: There are a lot of parking lots in this world, and probably more than a few where you live. As you're out driving around, take notice of the lines that delineate parking spaces. Are they doing a disappearing act? Look at the curbs. Has the no-parking curbside paint vanished? Then that parking lot is calling your name!

Go to a paint store and you will find sprayers designed just for parking lot painting. They range in price from around $100 up to thousands of dollars. Buy the best you can afford, but don't be alarmed if that isn't the top-of-the-line model. Start small and work your way up as your business grows.

Next, buy paint. Needless to say, this should be a high-quality exterior grade paint designed just for this purpose. Now you need some practice. Go to a business in your area and tell them you're launching a parking lot painting business in the area, and as an introduction to your service, you'll restripe his lot for free. Tell him that if he likes your work, the only payment you expect is that he tells other business owners about your service.

Most likely, he'll accept this offer gladly. So gather your equipment and your paint, and on one of the days he's closed for business, cordon off the area with rope or plastic streamers and get to work. (Oh, before you do, take a "before" picture. You can follow up with an "after" shot and then you'll have the beginnings of a portfolio to show prospective customers.)

Now, it goes without saying that you've read the instructions that came with the equipment very carefully and will follow directions to the letter. Right'? Right. Go slowly. Remember, you're just learning. And you want referrals from this freebie! Give the paint sufficient time to dry, then take down the barriers. If you've done your job well, the business owner will be very happy when he returns to open shop! Drop by shortly after he's arrived and ask if the work was satisfactory. If so, tell him you're glad he's pleased. Then give him a stack of your business cards or flyers and tell him you'd appreciate any referrals he might give you.

On your next prospecting call, you can now say "If you'd like to see an example of my work, I just restriped the parking lot for So-and-So down the street. Here are a few before and after shots. Or, of course, you can drive by, see it in person, and talk to Mr. Business Owner. "

With a little luck, this will become your first paying job. But what should you charge? Try calling parking lot painters in your area and ask for an estimate on a certain size parking lot. You may have a hard time finding someone who's doing this type of work. Wouldn't that be nice! That means the work's all yours! You can also try online or in the Yellow Pages of larger cities. You might be more likely to find parking lot painters there.

Now, go back to all those places whose parking lots were yelling "Help!" and give it to them. You're in business!

Tools and equipment needed:

- o   Cell phone with voicemail service turned on
- o   Trucker or trailer
- o   Razor knife
- o   Heavy-duty stapler
- o   Bid forms

Home insulation is a great business to get into, and like other businesses described in this book, it doesn't require a lot of money to get started. Every building is insulated during construction, and many older houses, which often have no insulation at all, need insulating as well.

Insulating a building is not a complicated business. But there are a few things you need to know. There are two basic types of insulation: batt insulation, which comes in rolls and is placed between the studs in walls and the rafters in ceilings; and blown (or loose) insulation,   which comes in bags, blocks, or bails and is blown into walls and ceilings using blowing equipment.

Batt insulation can be installed with nothing more than a utility knife (for cutting the pieces) and a heavy-duty stapler (for fastening the insulation to the studs). Installing blown insulation requires a blowing machine, which can be purchased for under $2,000. You can also sometimes borrow or rent these machines from the place you purchase insulation.

Check online or in the Yellow Pages under "Insulation" or ask the pros at your local building supply stores. If you have never done insulating work, you should learn as much as possible before you go after for that first job. One of the best ways to do that is to get a job at an insulating business already in existence. If that isn't possible, get as much information as possible by talking to the guys at your local building supply store.

To find insulating work, try placing an ad in the "Services Offered" section of the classifieds. You can also have a magnetic sign created for the side of your truck or trailer. But one of the best ways to find insulating work is through contractors. Go to construction sites in your area and ask for the contractor in charge. Tell him a little about your service and ask him if you can bid on the job. Submit your bid on a professional bid form, available at office supply stores or from your local printer.

Now about pricing: The cost of insulation service varies from one area to another, but it's usually on a square-foot basis. Insulators usually measure the areas to be insulated (walls, floors, ceilings, etc.) and charge so much per square foot. For example, if a house has 2,000 square foot of space to be insulated, you multiply 2,000 times the amount you will charge per square foot. This gives you your price.

To find out the going rate per square foot in your area, try getting a few estimates over the phone from competitors. So, you've set your rates and learned your craft. Now, go get those jobs. Do it right and an insulating business can "insulate" you from financial problems!

Tools and Equipment Needed:

- Cell phone with voicemail service turned on
- Roller handle
- Roller pads
- Five-foot extension stick
- Trim brush (2 1/2 to 3 inch)
- Buckets
- Bucket screen
- Sandpaper
- Painter's putty and knife
- Screwdrivers
- Drop cloths or plastic
- Bid forms

Painting is not difficult work. Virtually everyone can do it. Still, most busy home owners don't have the time or inclination to paint and are willing to pay good prices to someone who does.

To get started in the painting business, you must learn about paints. Latex. Oil-based. Interior. Exterior. Prime products. Finish products. Flat. Semi-gloss. There are literally hundreds of different products on the market. Go to the paint stores in your area and ask for a crash course. If they specialize in a particular line, ask them what makes their product superior to other products. (This will help you determine what line of paints you'll use in your business.) Plant yourself in the paint aisle of your local home improvement store and read the labels on the paint cans. You can't be a painter until you understand paint.

Second, you must purchase some equipment. Don't skimp, especially on brushes. Buy the best you can afford. A good angled brush will run at least $16 to $25.

Third, you must learn to paint. One of the best ways to do this is to work with an experienced painter. A few weeks of watching a pro should teach you the basics. You can pick up the more dramatic techniques (sponging, feathering, glazing, etc.) later by doing a little reading and practicing on your own.

As with other businesses, you must perfect your craft before you set out to pursue customers. Paint your house (inside and out). Paint your mother's house. Paint your friend's house. Even your mother-in-law's house. Let them supply the paint. You supply the labor. Six weeks of practice and you'll have your technique down.

Prices for painting vary widely from one area to another. Prices in my area generally run around $ .85 to $1.30 per square foot. So the cost of painting a 2,000-square- foot house might be around $1,700 to $2,600. Experienced painters with a wide client base can afford to charge more than someone just starting out. You may need to start at the bottom of the scale and raise your rates as you go along.

Charges for painting occupied spaces tend to run a little higher than those for new spaces, because the painter must move and/or protect items in the space (unless the occupant's volunteer to move everything for you). Novice painters should stick to new construction for a couple of years until their skills are honed.

Got your technique down? Your rates set? Then you're ready to pursue that first job. Go for something simple at first: a room or a couple of rooms. An addition. Start small, and as you gain confidence, go for more complex jobs.

One very important thing to remember: Used correctly, paint can beautify. Used incorrectly, it can really mess things up. So one of the first things you must do when you get to the job site is to cover every surface, every surface, that's not to be painted, with drop cloths or plastic. Don't skip this step! A few drops of paint on a thousand-dollar armoire or sofa and you—and your professional reputation—are history. Cover the floors too.

The second most important thing to remember is preparation. Proper preparation is the key to a professional result. Scrape off all loose paint. Fill all holes. Repair all cracks. Mud, sand, and spot-prime repaired areas. Remove all door and window hardware as well as switch and outlet covers. (Attach screws to these with a piece of tape so they don't get lost.)

Now you're ready to prime (if the surface has never been painted) and/or paint. Use only premium-quality products. Cheap stuff won't give you the result you're looking for, and it's harder to work with.

After you've "cut in" along the floors and ceiling with your angled brush, you're ready to roll—literally. Apply paint to walls with your paint roller, making a big "M" pattern with the first few strokes while your roller is loaded, then spreading the paint to a wider area. Go slowly. Rolling too fast causes the paint to splatter or mist. Clean up drips immediately with a damp rag you keep handy for this purpose. Latex paint cleans up easily with water if you get to it fast.

Don't leave off the finishing steps: Caulk around trim. Remove excess paint from windows. Reattach hardware, light switch covers, and plug covers. (If the covers are really old or ugly, replace them. They cost less than a dollar each, and this little extra service will boost your customer's satisfaction immensely.)

Now that you're a paint pro, you're ready to find customers. Try apartment complexes. They usually have frequent turnover and therefore need frequent painting. Consider offering the manager a service in which you not only paint walls, trim, and doors, but you also get the apartment in move-in condition. (See Chapter 15 for more information.)

Real estate companies usually manage several properties—condominiums as well as apartments—and are great places to find paint work. Simply go to the property manager and introduce yourself and your service and ask if you can bid on any existing work.

When you're bidding on a job, look the place over carefully. What needs to be done? Which surfaces will require semi-gloss paints and which will need flat? (Kitchens and baths and all wood trim are usually painted with high-gloss or semi-gloss, as these areas get dirty and need to be washable. Walls are usually painted with flat paint, which tends to downplay flaws.) Use your notes to prepare a bid.

Don't be discouraged if you don't score on your first few calls. Keep trying. The more calls you make, the better you will become at selling your service. But don't quit. A little persistence and a lot of good work, and a painting business can make your life a whole lot " greener"!

Tools and Equipment Needed:

- o Cell phone with voicemail service turned on
- o Scoop
- o Shop vacuum
- o Bucket
- o Chimney brushes
- o Brush rods
- o Wire brush (hand)
- o Flashlight
- o Pliers
- o Screwdriver
- o Dropcloth
- o Roll of plastic
- o Cotton gloves
- o Goggles
- o Hand cleaner
- o Ladder
- o Receipt book

This is dirty work, but it can be very profitable, particularly today, when more people are aware of the explosive danger of ash and creosote buildup in their chimneys. To be a chimney sweep, you'll need to invest in the appropriate brushes and rods. You should be able to get these at hardware stores in your town. If they don't have the equipment you need, they may be able to order it for you or tell you where to find it.

You should only need a couple of brushes. The most common are 11 x 11 inches and 11 x 13 inches. These sizes will fit most chimney flues, and the rods that connect to these brushes come in five-foot lengths and can be coupled together as needed to reach the full depth of the flue.

As with other businesses discussed in this book, you'll need to practice before you launch your chimney sweep business. Start with your own chimney, then clean the chimneys of a few relatives or friends.

To begin, bring your dropcloth into the home and place it over the hearth and as much of the surrounding area around as possible.

Now bring in your equipment: shop vacuum, bucket, everything except your ladder. Reach up inside the flue and close the damper. It usually has a handle that moves back and forth or up and down. Next, close off the front of the fireplace. Some fireplaces have glass doors. Close them and seal the edges with tape. This will ensure that soot and ashes don't enter the home when you begin to brush the inside of the flue. If there are no doors, seal the front of the fireplace with plastic and tape.

Once you've taken the proper precautions around the fireplace area, you're ready to clean the flue. Go outside and, using your ladder, climb up on the roof. Make sure you're wearing shoes with non-slick bottoms, and be very, very careful. Roofs can be slippery or have loose shingles that can send you toppling to the ground.

Carefully make your way over to the flue and remove the cap if it has one. Using your wire brush, scrape the cap to remove ash buildup, then lay it aside in a secure place near the chimney. Next, connect the proper size brush to one five-foot section of the brush rod and start brushing up and down inside the flue. Start at the top and gradually work your way deeper and deeper into the flue. After you have brushed down approximately five feet, add another section of rod. Proceed with this until you have reached the bottom. You will know this has happened when brushing suddenly becomes easy. Take your time with this step and do it well.

When you've finished brushing, use your flashlight and inspect the flue for damage (cracks or chips). If you find such damage, report this information to the home owner. (He or she may ask you for the name of a good mason, so if you know anyone, take the phone number along for such occasions.)

Now replace the cap and make your way back down the ladder. If you haven't already done so, you'll need to put on some old clothing or coveralls. Go into the house and carefully open the fireplace door or remove the plastic you used to seal the opening. Using your scoop and bucket, remove all the ashes and wood from the fireplace. Move slowly throughout this procedure to prevent soot and ash from spreading throughout the room. Now slowly open the damper. You may need to pull the pin from the damper hinges to do this. Using your shop vacuum—just the hose, no attachments—vacuum everything you can reach around the damper.

Now, this is the dirty part. You must position yourself inside the fireplace with your back against the fireplace wall, looking out to the room. Then you should take your vacuum hose and, reaching over your shoulder, vacuum the fire shelf. Once this is complete, slowly remove yourself from the fireplace and replace the damper.

Next, using your wire brush and vacuum, clean all the fireplace walls. When you're absolutely sure you've cleaned every surface and any flying ash has settled, carefully fold your drop cloth in such a way as to keep all debris contained and carry it outside for emptying in the garbage bag or container you've brought for this purpose. Then take out all your tools and equipment.

Now you're ready to go to your vehicle, where you've stored hand cleaner and rags, and clean yourself up as well as possible. If you've donned coveralls over your clothes for the dirtier parts of the job, you might want to slip those off.

Now go collect your pay! The entire job should take 45 minutes to an hour and a half and net you $75 to $150!

A word about marketing. Three avenues seem to work best: a social media ad under "Chimney Sweeps," an ad in the "Services Offered" sections of newspapers in your area, and a magnetic sign on your vehicle announcing your service. You could also drive into various neighborhoods and look for chimneys. Tape a business card or hang a flyer on the door of every house with a chimney. Do this at enough houses and your phone will ring!

Yes, it's a "dirty" business, but the pay is great. So if you're willing to get dirty, you can really clean up!

Tools and Equipment Needed:

- o Cell phone with voicemail service turned on
- o Cleaning supplies (window, bath, and wood cleaners)
- o Brooms (push and regular)
- o Dust mop
- o Wet mop and bucket
- o Carpet cleaning equipment
- o Roller handle
- o Roller pads
- o Five-foot extension stick
- o Trim brush (2 1/2 to 3 inch)
- o Hammer
- o Paint bucket
- o Bucket screen
- o Sandpaper
- o Painter's putty and knife
- o Screwdrivers
- o Drop cloths or plastic
- o Bid forms

This is a great service that's sure to make you a lot of money, and it doesn't have to cost a lot to get started. In case you're unfamiliar with the term, "turnkey" refers to the completion of a job from start to finish.

"Rental units" can refer to houses, apartments, or condominiums. When a tenant moves out of any kind of rental unit, it inevitably needs sprucing up for the next occupant. Generally, the property owner or manager has to call a janitorial service to come in and clean, a painting contractor to come in and paint, and a carpet cleaner to come in and clean the carpets.

But if you offer a complete, or turnkey, service, the property owner or manager makes only one phone call--to you. You come in and do al/ these services, saving the owner or manager time and money and vastly simplifying his or her work.

If you're interested in launching this business, you should refer to Chapters one and thirteen. These chapters will give your more information about the painting and cleaning aspects of this service.

An important note about carpet cleaning: Unless you can afford top-of-the-line equipment, it's best to leave this job to a pro. Over-the-counter equipment just doesn't do the job. To find a professional carpet cleaner, check online or in the Yellow Pages under "Carpet Cleaners" or "Janitorial Services." Be sure to ask for the commercial rate. Most carpet cleaners offer a discount on commercial work. You should also ask for references.

Once you've chosen a good carpet cleaning service, you're ready to go get that first rental unit. Most property owners or managers are very open to this type of service, as it will save them time and headaches, so it should be an easy sell. Emphasize your reliability and your willingness to respond quickly to their call. Let them know that you understand a rental unit loses money every day it's vacant, and you can have it ready to occupy again in short order. Remind them that with just one call to you the job will be taken care of—start to finish.

Pricing a turnkey service like this can be a little tricky. Try to find out what it's costing the property owner or manager to turn a unit using separate services. Then tell him or her that you believe you can do it for less. Ask to see the vacant unit. Note the size, age, and condition and use this information to prepare your bid. Take your time. Make your bid reasonable, but don't sell your work too cheaply. It's difficult or impossible to raise your price once you've quoted the job.

Something else to remember: When you're looking the property over to prepare your bid, keep your eye out for additional work that needs to be done: holes that need repaired, carpet that needs restretched, etc. These represent opportunities or additional work, over and on top of your normal spruce-up.

No, you won't get a job from everyone you talk to. But one good-sized realtor or apartment complex can set you up nicely. So get out there and make those calls. Spruce up some rentals, and you can spruce up your bank account!

Regardless of the business you choose to start, there are certain things that you should do to ensure its success.

1. <u>When you're calling on a prospect, dress neatly and appropriately.</u> A suit generally isn't necessary, but you should wear clean, well-pressed clothing. Your shoes should be polished and in good repair. Your hair and nails should be clean and neatly trimmed. Look like someone with whom a prospect would want to do business.

2. <u>Mind your manners</u>. Unless you're invited to, don't call your prospect by his or her first name. Use Mr. or Mrs., or sir or ma'am. Excuse yourself upon entering your prospect's office if there's a chance you may be interrupting his or her work. Extend you hand and introduce yourself upon meeting. Never use offensive or foul language, no matter how well you think you know the client.

3. <u>Learn your customer's name</u>. And use it often. Dale Carnegie's book How to Win Friends and Influence People taught us this long ago: People love the sound of their own names. So pay attention when your prospect tells you his or her name. Immediately repeat it back to him in a sentence or question to enhance your chances of remembering it. And once you're back in your vehicle, write it down. Refer to your notes whenever you call on that customer.

4. <u>Always make sure your potential customers can contact you.</u> It's critical that you have a cell phone with voicemail service turned on to catch calls when you're not available. They've dropped in cost considerably over the past few years, so virtually everyone can afford one. Two important points about these communication tools: One, make sure the message on your voicemail sounds professional. This is no place to practice a standup comedy routine. So skip the jokes. Forego the riffs from your favorite tunes too. Keep your message professional, and brief: "This is (the name of your business). I'm sorry we're not available to take your call right now, but please leave a message and we'll return your call as soon as possible. Thank you." Second, if you have a message, return the call promptly. Immediately, if possible. If that isn't possible, make a note of the number and return the call as quickly as possible. Calls not returned are business lost!

5. <u>Be-honest</u>. It will pay off in the long run. For example, if your client overpays you, go to him or her and report that. You'll earn their respect, and undoubtedly their future business as well.

6. <u>Price your service competitively.</u> If you price your service too low, potential customers may think your work is inferior. If you price it too high, you'll have a problem getting work at all. Research existing rates carefully and price your service accordingly.

7. <u>Never be afraid to ask questions.</u> Find out as much as you can about the business in general and about each job in particular. The more questions you ask, the more answers you get, and the more you'll know.

8. <u>Always perform quality work.</u> Quality work not only establishes your reputation as a professional, it inevitably leads to more work. Which means more money. Which is one of the biggest reasons you go into business for yourself in the first place.

9. <u>Advertise your business in as many ways as you can.</u> Don't neglect this important step. It doesn't matter how terrific your service is if no one knows it exists.

10. <u>Support your business with the appropriate print materials.</u> This includes business cards, flyers, and occasionally, brochures. If you can't afford advertising agency prices, try to find independent writers and designers who can do the project for you. (Check the online or in the Yellow Pages, or ask agencies if they know someone who specializes in working with low-budget clients.) You can also try the communications department at your local college or university, where talented students will often do the job at a fraction of the cost.
11. <u>Don't give up.</u> So many small business owners quit just as things are about to break for them. If you're not succeeding, take a long look at what you might be doing wrong and try to do it differently. Ask advice from people whose business savvy you respect. Regroup. Then keep going.
12. <u>Believe in yourself.</u> Cliché as it is, if you don't, no one else will.

For additional copies of this book or information about ordering future editions describing more easy-to-start businesses, call 1-800-825-3596. This book was edited by Debbie Smith Denton, a freelance writer and editor living in Clarksville, Tennessee.

If you need professional, affordable editorial assistance with your project, write or call:

Debbie Smith Denton 410 Greenwood Ave.
Clarksville, Tennessee 37040
(615) 647-1590
Cover Design by Carlin Design
(615) 648-2095